follow your heart

To Grace.

By following . . .
May you find the land
where your heart truly
dwells.

Walter Rinder

The best of my

love . . . . Dave

Summer of '75

Celestial Arts
Millbrae, California 94030

First Printing, August 1973
Second Printing, November 1973
Third Printing, February 1974
Library of Congress Card No. 73-82332
ISBN 0-912310-39-1
Made in the United States of America

I know the sun will rise every morning,

even when there is fog.

I know the

whippoorwills sing melodious songs

because

I have heard them from the

enclosure of my room.

I know the sky is blue-looking through the haze,

that the

grass is green,

even when I stand in the

desert.

I know the branches of trees dance

to the movements of the wind,

even though now

it is still.

I know flowers have

beautiful smells,

that the ocean

never sleeps

and that snow

falls upon high

mountains.

I know deeply

that all living things

are as important to this earth

as I am,

that all things are beautiful,

if they are born free

to follow their hearts.

It has been said,

long before these written words,

that if you build an archway

for your heart,

with neither lock nor door,

life will pass freely in harmony with

your senses.

TOUCH

. . . your friends,

your lover,

a stranger,

then they are a stranger no more.

Hold them,

feel the beauty of

their skin,

their face,

their hair...

as

you would touch

the delicate petals of

a carnation

or put your hand in a

gentle stream

or feel the sand

beneath your feet

or climb upon the rocks and

crags of the shoreline.

LISTEN

> *. . . to their words,*

> *their breathing,*

> *their heartbeat,*

their footsteps on the

carpet of leaves as they

come to you . . .

as you would listen to the

rain, or

the deer running through

the forest,

or the bark of a dog,

or the cascading of

a waterfall, or

a tiny breeze.

SEE

... on their faces

   the expressions

of their different moods.

See in their eyes

the longing for love,

companionship

and a meaningful purpose to

their lives.

See their bodies move,

    uniting themselves with

        life.

See their hands

create their inner being...

as you would see a tidepool,

the splash of a wave,

a new portrait made by falling

snow,

the landscape of a valley,

the changing

of a sunset.

SPEAK

. . . to them of love,

of the harmony of nature,

of quiet understanding

among men,

of the simple things in

life in which one can

find peace, of the

truth you have found...

as you would speak to God.

Ride the crest of the wave

to the shore.

Follow the river till it merges with the

ocean.

Look at the clouds till they

disappear.

Watch the sun rise...

its path

across the sky,

then vanish.

When you have experienced these things

you will

know your heart...

follow it.